AF412210

LIFT UP THY VOICE

LIFT UP THY VOICE

M. Moore Williams

Philosophical Library
New York

Library of Congress Cataloging in Publication Data

Williams, M. Moore.
    Lift up thy voice.

    1. Aphorisms and apothegms.   I. Title.
PN6271.W65   1984   081   83-25044
ISBN 0-8022-2426-1

Manufactured in the United States of America

To
My Beloved Wife, Margaret,
who retrieved these writings from a dark shelf

PREFACE

As a casual reader you might like to know that this book does not contain curse words, obscenity, sex or violence. If these be what you seek, then look elsewhere.

This book does cause the imagination to speculate, gives pleasure and companionship, and gentle mental exercise. It should help banish the worries that arise with daily troubles.

Open this book at random and consider what you find. Now, if you will, lay the book down, pick it up, and again open it at random, pause and consider this.

Congratulations if this is your first experience in the field of literature generally classified as philosophical.

Teachers and students of philosophy, hopefully, will find some original phrasing and possibly a new presentation which can be used as source material.

This work has provided the writer with pleasure for more than a quarter of a century in its composing; and some of this can be shared by a discerning reader.

The title is taken from King Solomon's lecture to his son on living, being in Proverbs, second chapter, paragraph three, and is, of course, taken carefully. While it is not intended that this should be a religious book, using the common definition of religion, it does deal with the powers that be and the methods of power application and guidance.

It has been impossible to define good and bad, short and long, right and wrong, justice and injustice, lie and truth, and such situations with a precision that can stand exact analysis. Therefore a definition has been found and used, which is the meaning commonly used by all and which has arisen from human experience and understanding.

This human experience seems to be the true solver of all relationships, religion and good will; and such an answer comes from the experience of thousands through a period of time which must be called lengthy. These thousands will find all weak bridges as they tread their paths and will cry out in alarm.

There being such a great volume of material, brevity became imperative, presented by a variant format.

TO THE READER

Let him who studies beware of the printer who uses unskilled labor, the grammarian with many commas, and the professor who must speak for hours.

These take nothing from the many, are an oddity at the worst; and to the ones who follow with me, GREETINGS, and a request. Seek other avenues, and if you find none, retrace these as they are cool, stand alone each in its own beauty, and the fruits are delicious and mostly unplucked.

And thus you come to the beginning of these, and there were those written and discarded, possibly better, and there are others not written but lost as yet.

ABUSE

When you come to the end of a trail, yet you can cut further; to the end of a rope, you can tie on additional rope—yet when a man dies, if you have abused him, you cannot make amends.

[6-4-59]

ACCEPTANCE

Ye smart ones who fear greatly accept, accept, accept, accept, though there is some consolation in doing what you may.

[4-15-57]

ACCLAIM

A seeker of small acclaim wears a cocked hat with a feather.

[6-19-63]

ACTIVITY

Act hastily or not at all and remorse will gnaw in the belly; and like most belly pains, will pass, but more slowly.

[11-3-64]

~

Activity without wisdom produces sweat and bruised knuckles—wisdom without activity is an abomination.

[4-7-75]

~

12 *ACTIVITY*

For those who act, the opportunities for profit and pleasure are uncountable; but for him who sits and does nothing there shall be nothing and he shall also mourn his bad fate.

[6-16-78]

~

Some successes have been had in efforts to identify and overcome the factors limiting all activity, and these have brought forth outcries of "fool" and "genius."   [12-31-79]

ADVERSITY

While heated by the blows of adversity, be not moulded by temptation.   [8-11-56]

~

Lashes of adversity make a tough hide, and the prosperous have shoes and cannot longer go barefooted on the hard ground.   [12-18-58]

ADVICE

Bad advice is a weak bridge; and if you would first test a bridge, test advice.   [3-2-58]

~

Offer a man a snake, and he takes it slowly; and give him advice and he takes it twice as slowly as a snake.   [10-18-60]

AFFECTION

Affection cannot be stored, it cannot be seized, though it may enlarge by sharing.   [2-17-61]

AGING

No one fears for the aging man, and all regret his white hairs, plain to see.   [7-6-57]

~

Old ivory and judgment improve with aging.   [1-21-58]

~

A lion growls and you seek a tree; a grey hair comes to your head, and you pluck it out.   [7-23-58]

~

It is the older who are given pure sorrow.   [9-18-58]

~

Walk not on the Earth as on thin ice, count not your later days, for you cannot, and this consumes a part.   [1-19-59]

~

A vineyard has a time of full ripeness; and the years of a man from 40 to 60 are the period of the ripe grape.   [5-4-60]

~

The skin between your eyebrows can wrinkle as an old coat.   [12-11-61]

~

This is no cause for sorrow or surprise—an old wood-chopper is not hired to cut down a large tree.   [9-23-64]

~

An old man finds his glory in the newborn day. [11-25-64]

AID
Another step—aid one another.   [6-24-80]

ALARM
Call out in alarm thrice unduly, and it will place you in the dunce box, and it will cost you dignity to come forth thence.   [7-28-61]

ALONE
Alone you stand, alone you will be, and you cannot be part of another, nor of many.   [3-3-75]

AMBITION
A lion desires not to be an elephant, yet man aspires to something greater.   [10-25-60]

~

Let not ambition beat thee as a rider beats his mount.
[6-15-60]

~

The foul ones seek the seats of leadership, as the moth seeks a flame; and the foul ones can ruin a nation before truth consumes them as the flame consumes the moth.   [11-2-62]

ANGELS

Limitations are placed on the angels in their relation to men: and these are not on a tablet.   [9-15-56]

~

If the angels jest with you, indeed you are a happy one.
[6-25-57]

~

There is a wall without beginning, without an end, unclimbable, and without a gate, and I cannot know if there be a new angel.   [2-8-58]

~

In the rocks, in the books, in the memory of men there is recorded not a single footprint of an angel.   [12-7-58]

ANGER

An idiot calls thee an idiot and opens a book on himself; and if he angers you, he is partly right.   [10-27-58]

~

Iron lying in the air rusts; and one, who is angered, speaks loudly; and this is as the rust upon the iron.   [9-16-59]

~

He who yields to anger must first hurt himself.   [8-19-75]

~

The whistle of a high-flying bird deserves more attention than harsh words spoken in haste or anger.   [1-19-78]

~

Act not in anger—anger blinds the eyes and you cannot know if things are truly red.   [10-20-60]

ANGUISH

Anguish comes slowly and smallishly from others—quickly and neatly from yourself.   [10-15-56]

APPLAUSE

A gentle breeze blows through a pecan tree and maketh a pleasant noise; and the pecans fall for all; and the applause of an audience is a pleasant noise and they drop their pennies and a pecan sprouts and lasteth.   [1-24-58]

APPROVAL

An early bird finding not a seed, flyeth off. A beautiful woman combs her hair and sandals well her feet and walks forth, and finding not an approving eye, walks elsewhere.
[7-5-63]

ART

The artist paints a picture a stroke at a time, and it is not better than the least; and so it is with your each and every step.
[5-1-59]

~

Be a maker of fine art—secure a sheet of white paper, some free sunlight and place your hand in the light casting a shadow on the paper; and you will find a purity of line alone in all time, and the picture separate, new and never to be repeated.
[3-7-62]

ASSAULT

If a thief assault you with a weapon, yield, for there is no better answer.   [4-27-60]

ASSETS

As assets and knowledge are distributed more evenly, so do accomplishments and success level and become more even.
[1-13-75]

ATTRACTION

The peel of an apple is pretty and catches the eye; and if aught attracts, consider the peeling of an apple.   [1-19-59]

BACTERIA

Bacteria are an alien form of life and wage war without malice or mercy, a war that has few generals and heroes, yet victims beyond counting, and the counting has not yet ended.
[12-21-79]

BEAUTY

To see the color of the leaves in the Fall, one must look in the Fall; to see the red shafts of dawn, one must look to the East; to see the beauties of change one can look anywhere at any time, and these beauties cause the color of the leaves to fade and the red shafts to dim.   [10-6-61]

~

For this day—beauty beyond man—fresh and free for all— look at dawn and sunset—and forget not the night's rest.
[9-18-62]

~

How beautiful is the family where the father tells what each shall do;

How beautiful is a city in the valley when you know of the trash gatherers;

How beautiful is a nation of many cities when the power of unity is known;

How beautiful is the struggle for a common understanding by all men this day!

How terrible is the menace if the power seekers grab this struggle for a common understanding.   [8-20-63]

~

Roll upon the grass, look up at the sky and take with thee a moment of beauty.   [12-6-64]

BEING
The loss of each being is felt by the whole of the world.   [12-12-56]

BELIEF
We pick and choose from what was produced during the preceding 10,000 orbits of the Sun; and we believe that during the next revolution of the Earth there will be a little, just a very little, more produced from which to pick and choose.[8-3-80]

BIRTH
Propagate and build highways that feet may hurry and wheels roll, for these crumble not as a broken cracker.   [9-13-56]

~

Procreation is for the sound of body and mind. [10-10-56]

~

The glow of dawn beautifies the coming day; the blossom on the tree points the place of the fruit; and so it is as a baby is born.   [5-1-58]

~

You cannot choose birth, yet much more there is that you may choose to choose.   [6-26-61]

BLAME
If another does a wrong, and you are blamed, you will have the help of many; if you do a wrong and another is blamed, you stand alone and have no help.   [5-31-60]

BODY
A body served by eating, drinking and breathing is served insufficiently, crudely and dangerously.   [1-13-75]

Take care of thy body and all its parts, keep all clean, and well groomed; and rewards will come as a gentle breeze in the night.   [6-3-78]

BORROWING

Borrow not, for this is bad, but repay fast, for this is good; but borrow not again, nor break a plate twice.   [5-1-58]

BREATH

At birth first you breathe freely, then you lastly breathe, and nothing has a greater value; and so two lines appear—cost and value.   [6-3-64]

BREATHING

Breathe deeply, and again, until you can breathe no more, thus easily you find a door beyond which you may not go.   [8-1-61]

BRIBES

A bribe giver and a bribe taker stab each other.   [4-6-59]

BROTHERS

Your brother is alone, and the people of China are a people; and both concepts be right.   [5-22-62]

BUILDING

Take clay, which is there, and fire, and make a brick and build a house, for surely the winds must blow.   [3-25-58]

BURDENS

Each shall have his burdens, and many larger and larger, and he is known.   [10-15-57]

BURIAL

A job the living owe the dead, is burial; and be it a loved one

or a stranger, soon array the body with usual raiment, buying
nothing new; dig a place of proper depth, covering the body
with a light cloth, and the face; lower the body with ropes,
regain the ropes, and gently fill with soft soil. Level and plant
grass and mark with a small cross of branches, lest the marker
last and so make the body an exhibit and it lose its full return,
and take a part of ground from those who yet have need of it.
[2-14-59]

CARE

Place not idly a grain of sand on your head for its carrying
may exhaust you and you might not do what you should; and
step thy step with care, for you have so many and no more.
[4-11-58]

CHALLENGE

Stamp on the ground, hurl a spear and nothing challenges,
except another.   [4-25-58]

CHANCE

The laws of chance vary not, and apply not to labor assigned
to each.   [10-3-60]

CHANGE

A zebra cares not to change its stripes and cannot; but you
do, and can.   [1-10-59]

~

That which was and is containeth good—so it is good that
men strong in body, mind and character possess vast proper-
ties; but the rule that all changes is superior.   [6-1-64]

CHARACTER

A pod has peas and they are about the same, so it is with
character and spirit.   [2-9-56]

~

Form character first—it is first, and needs study and a strong mold.   [9-11-56]

~

To change your character: In a night, listen to your heart—take your finger and feel the blood pressure in the big arteries in the neck—count the beats for a minute—multiply by 60—then 24—then times 365, a year.

You cannot remain the same.   [6-24-80]

CHARITY

Charity begets good and evil; and is best done by the poor.   [4-1-78]

~

Enforced charity is a tax and hath supporters and detractors and interferes with the distribution of wealth.   [2-2-59]

~

The light of day exceeds the light of night; and the giving of charity by the poor exceeds the giving of charity by the rich as the light of the day exceeds the light of night.   [2-2-60]

~

Wasted charity is like a brown calf, not rare.   [6-19-60]

CHEERFULNESS

Man eats of the fruit and hath the Sun, and he pays for these in part by cheerfulness.   [11-28-60]

CHILDREN

All know to teach children of the things that be. [7-16-55]

~

A child's dependency on its father and mother forms the family; interfere not.   [4-24-57]

~

A child rattleth a toy, and the symphonies are stilled.

[9-14-58]

~

Parental defects are passed on to the children who wash the defects away with tears of anguish.   [11-2-78]

CHOICE

Choose, choose and choose, for you must, not knowing; and welcome the tiger, for things come.   [10-30-57]

~

You come placed, and there are places on mountains, places in valleys, and places, many places, so you may choose, for you must have a place, and having chosen, as you may, choose yet again, if you like, but finally choose, and soon.   [10-29-58]

~

You may skin a cow with your teeth or with a knife, you have a choice; and the choice comes from the making of the knife.
                                                     [2-5-60]

~

An exercise—there be those who bake and those who eat and choose the one who has the better of this.   [11-16-60]

CLEANLINESS

Plow in a field and you will be muddy; build a house and sweat will stain thy shirt; cry, "All out to clean the streets," and criticism as an oil will be poured on thy head; but mud, sweat and oil wash away and you are clean again.   [11-3-64]

CLIMATE

Some calculations seem worthwhile, as to the power to which engines can be built which can be fueled from the earth's resources; and raising the possibility that such engines could safely alter the earth's rotation; and whether such engines could alter the earth's attitude as it continues its monotonous orbit of the Sun and thus alter the climate.   [1-30-79]

CONDITIONS

Conditions always improve, and those around you have not been better, but will be.   [4-10-62]

CONFIDENCE

Clouds and silver and honor come slowly and fast and stay awhile and leave slowly and fast, and this gives confidence.
[10-14-57]

CONSCIENCE

A blind pilot cannot take a ship into a rocky harbor in a dense fog at night, nor can conscience guide you on a broad plain at high noon on a sunny day. [3-29-59]

CONSOLATION

The poor are consoled for they fear not the theft of an ermine coat—they are consoled as they can sit in the shade of a mango tree, eat fully and idly pick the ticks from their hair. [8-24-74]

CONTROL

You can control a team of eight horses, even turbulent waters; but you cannot control another, even a child, for it is not for you. [5-1-59]

CONTROLS

The controls over the life pattern are sure, lasting, and strong; and compare with gravity for importance. [2-4-80]

COURAGE

Shoe well your feet, and this will serve better than great courage. [1-29-58]

CRIME

Man's justice is incomplete, it taketh not into account the stars.

Statistics show that more crimes were committed when there was a brilliant full moon, and during the long days of summer.

Thus the impact of light from the Sun acted as an outside factor without which these extra crimes would not have been committed. Due allowance should be made for this influence, yet the law and courts do not do this.   [5-15-55]

~

Crime comes only from an intelligent level.   [11-2-78]

~

There is a crime becoming worse; and that is for a man to beget children when he has no spring from which to secure water, nor land to produce food.   [8-3-80]

CRUELTY

A lion's cruelty is no cruelty; but that of the sword is pure.   [12-23-60]

CRYING

Cry out in happiness—cry out in alarm when danger is near, and these gain you a pat on the back; and cry not out in pain and this gains you a pat on the back and a piece of cake.   [10-30-58]

CURSING

Go you first into a large vacant field, if you damn and curse and give forth loud noises, and drag not another's name into this mess.   [9-23-57]

CUSTOMS

Customs nestle comfort and respectability, while slowing social and economic growth.   [1-9-57]

~

Custom is a stone bridge built to cross a stream which in time runs dry.   [9-14-58]

~

Beware of customs for they harbor abuses, and are as a basket of fruit, not all good.   [3-15-60]

DANGER

Plan for dangers, for you have them; and there is that which you may do.   [7-24-57]

~

Danger lies in the improving of the bodies of men, as surely a super-intelligent one will come who has a lust for power.   [2-1-75]

~

We walk forth daily into unknown dangers that can assail and destroy—yet there are fewer than there were and all will be known and ended.   [9-25-78]

DARKNESS

Day is done and darkness comes, and this you know; but darkness lasts until the sun cometh, and there is darkness save where light is given.   [12-23-58]

DAYS

All your years will not be prosperous, all the days will not be happy ones; but each day is a triumph and you have nothing better.   [3-11-64]

DEATH

Having gone, none can return.   [5-27-55]

~

Death is provident, for it giveth to some and taketh nothing from any.   [1-16-56]

~

There is a quiet acceptance of death by us who are.   [8-17-56]

~

The people die idly, perish miserably and know not what they do—there is a lack.   [9-25-56]

~

Man may seek the reason for death, beyond the knife.
[2-16-57]

~

Study the pattern of death, that you may change your pace
and place, if you will. [2-16-57]

~

A woman must prepare herself to see her man die, for he first
completes that which he does—and one may thus find another
line in the pattern. [4-9-57]

~

Look to the Sun and clouds, look around you, for the death
of a loved one carried but a portion of you. [5-18-57]

~

Mourn as you may upon the loss of a friend, mourn as you
do but for a day, for this is measured—let not your mourning
last longer than the flowering of the lilly. [5-18-57]

~

And you buy milk, and it is soured, you gain naught; and you
buy eggs, and they are rotten, you lose; and you buy of the
seller of the fear of death, you gain naught. [11-1-59]

DEBRIS
On the back trail is the debris of many things and that which
is left is shiny and of high value. [7-28-61]

DEBTS
A drop of water overweighs a child's debt. [8-27-58]

DECEIT
A dark cloud yields hail, tornadoes, and much woe, and
deceit is as a dark cloud. [9-2-64]

DEEDS
Slice an apple and you say, "This is the right half—and this is
the left half"; and either is either: a man does a deed and you say

"brave" or "foolish" and this remains the apple sliced and the deed done.   [4-25-58]

~

A bird passes quickly in flight, and so it is with the opportunity to do a good thing for a loved one or a stranger; that you may earn a gem in your crown, seize the chance, seize the chance, and do it fully and freely.   [2-14-59]

~

Each thing that is in the morning sunshine has a fine shadow; and each deed has a shadow all its own.   [6-3-60]

DEFENSE

A man can lift only a small horse, and the defense of yourself is a large horse.   [2-10-60]

DEPENDENCE

Lean upon your father and mother, and lean upon a stranger if you must.   [9-19-58]

DEPRIVATION

A reproved child makes a better man, better workers come from the poor; and take much from a man and he knows better what is left.   [12-19-60]

DESIRE

Build not on the hot desire, for surely it will cool, and cooling will shrink.   [12-19-56]

~

Know what you desire of your friends, lest you seem as a cat creeping in the shadows of a moonlit night.   [8-22-60]

DESTINATIONS

The coat maker obtains his cloth from the clothmaker; and men do their deeds from a guiding hand; and the destination is not a set course.   [8-13-59]

DESTRUCTION

Destroy and despoil not that which is here, for the penalty exceeds thy strength. [4-11-57]

DETRACTORS

A coyote howls a mournful cry in the dark, and you can tread the dirt of a path firmly; and if a detractor speak badly of you, it is not more than a coyote howl, so tread the dirt of the path firmly. [6-16-69]

DEVASTATION

Voices are heard through the land proclaiming devastation from the voracious consumption of the plant and animal life and other vital elements. [7-4-78]

DEVIOUSNESS

Iron is hard, water runs down a hill, and devious schemes entangle their owner. [10-22-58]

DIFFERENCES

The two hands and feet be about the same, and the nose, yet the color of hair and eyes mattereth not; but a difference that matters between one and another lies in what each is willing to serve for his wants. [6-28-61]

DOING

First comes worth and usefulness in all there is that you find to do. [5-27-55]

~

Do that which you do as in the open, for it is; and you cannot hide within yourself that which you would hide—a light gloweth there. [5-27-55]

~

For a list, write that which men do that men alone can do. [1-25-56]

Use that which you have, lest it be given to another.

[2-19-56]

~

Go forth, the affairs of men are not in human hands, and if you stumble, you are strengthened.   [3-22-56]

~

While the wind whistles an idle tune, dance and prance on the earth as a stage, with the sun and floating clouds, and forget not the audience.   [9-13-56]

~

Do with what you have what you can, and your limitations come forth.   [5-15-57]

~

Salute not the hero of hasty action, for he is an accident; but applaud the deliberate man for he acts with steady courage.   [6-14-57]

~

Take alarm in what you do lest you seem what you are not.   [6-19-57]

~

Go as far as you can, and be not discouraged, for common honesty is depthless.   [7-10-57]

~

A simple problem, aid or harm thee any or aught by doing or not doing.   [4-7-59]

~

There are things that you can do, there are things that you must do, and these are paired as a fine team.   [6-10-60]

~

Take one step and the picture of all things changes, and you do no small thing.   [11-18-60]

~

When you are born, you owe for all; when you grow, the obligations mount; but comes a day and you can pay, with ease, and you may not know.   [12-13-60]

~

This is a bog, this is a swamp, this is a morass—do not as
others do because others do—this is a bog.   [9-12-62]

~

Do what you do so that it need not be redone until needs be,
and needs be will be.   [9-21-62]

~

You know not what you can do this day, nor your neighbor;
and that which you can freely do with that which is around you
may be the greatest privilege.   [1-14-64]

DREAMS

We laughed and played, ate the best we could find or make,
and dreamed of travelling through the great universe.

[9-13-56]

DUST

New weapons must be found in the struggle with dust, lest it
cover all.   [4-10-80]

EARTH

And the Earth spins and the wall is higher;
And the Earth spins and the wheat is fuller;
And the Earth spins and the workers go;
And the Earth spins and new hands lay brick.   [12-27-57]

~

A baby needs his milk warmed, but the Earth was not
prepared for men as warmed milk.   [2-15-60]

~

The spinning of the Earth needs halting—its dependence on
the sun's light needs abating—and its voyage in space be no
more and it be brought to a safe resting place.   [8-9-61]

~

Beware of this: Land, sea and air are limited, and as the
Earth becomes a city, beware of this.   [1-9-64]

~

Burn your coat in a breeze that carries the smoke so that it is lost; scatter the ashes that the Earth be not harmed—do this when your coat is worn and serves no longer.   [1-16-64]

~

Man, dig a hole—pave it so that heavy carts can pass—dig it to the center of the Earth for you may and it is not forbidden.   [9-29-74]

EATING

He who rides on a tall horse in a purple coat with many colors shall find his meat too salty.   [9-24-58]

~

Put a red bean in a pot of red beans and cook them, well spiced, and this will feed you and yours, and each day, do a red bean's worth or more.   [10-10-58]

~

Wrap a viper around your wrist, and if it bite you, yet you may live; but build a big stomach and it surely will kill you.   [2-23-59]

~

Put not poison, polluted water and overly fat foods in your belly, better a dagger thrust.   [7-7-61]

~

The poor and the rich mingle; and one has cake and the other bread made of corn, and the bread of corn is better for the body.   [1-4-62]

~

A roaring lion eats but little.   [4-8-63]

~

He who eats from the table of a foul man shall gnaw bones as a dog.   [7-31-63]

~

Eat of the bread and know the grain came from a field, eat of the savory meat and laugh at the law "eat and be eaten."   [10-22-74]

EFFORTS
It is true that your own efforts govern to a large degree your ultimate place in the scheme of things.   [8-26-78]

EMERGENCIES
Two emergencies confront all: the need for continued oxygen intake, and the never ceasing flood of blood in the body—and both can be eliminated.   [6-3-78]

EMOTION
A ship upon the sea uses the breezes; and the emotions of your friends are as the breezes of the sea.   [11-8-60]

ENDS
There is no surplus in the great oceans, there is no shortage of sand in a desert, and these lead to no end.   [10-27-60]

ENDURANCE
Speak a noise as a word, walk in the sun and cast a shadow on the grass; but if you would endure, make a small ball of wisdom and paint it red.   [11-15-58]

~

Two and two are four, three and nine are twelve, and these endure, but little else.   [12-30-59]

ENEMIES
A king without an enemy is an iron collar.   [12-20-57]

~

Two enemies you may have, one who injured you, and the one whom you have hurt; and of the two, run from the first.
[1-4-62]

~

He is an enemy of many who injures transportation, the opportunity for a profit, or the soundness of money.
[12-3-64]

ENVY

The wicked envy the good. [12-14-56]

~

You seek not the lash of a whip on thy back, nor seek the envy of others for this is as many lashes from a whip.
[12-23-64]

ERROR

If you place a brick in a wall awry, and it lasts for all to see, be not disconsolate for many live in the jungles and their scratchings in the dirt wash out with the next rain. [10-3-61]

ETHICS

He who carries chaff, shall go unpaid; he who saves chaff shall fill his room with nothing. [8-7-57]

~

A steel helmet, bad manners, and bad grammar are all heavy, cost much, and serve little; and of these the steel helmet is least heavy, costs less, and serves most. [6-14-60]

EVIL

He who does you evil and walks away has a cloudy face, walks in a ditch, and shall have a snake bite. [1-6-58]

~

And a man do you evil, first give him a chance to forgive.
[3-17-58]

EXHAUST

A cricket gives forth a noise, and is still a cricket; and a criminal gives forth a loud excuse, which only he finds of any use. [6-2-59]

EXPERIENCE

Secret factors impact our affairs, and are best measured by experience. [3-20-80]

FACTS

A small bridge carries not a large load; and build not great conclusions on small facts.   [4-8-60]

FAITH

The investiture of the Earth proceeds more rapidly, and when it reaches a maximum, the large demand for human labor shall diminish.   [12-1-79]

FAMILY

You spill your milk on the ground, you throw your bread to the birds, you cast off your clothes and burn them and stand bare, you who forsake your family.   [11-21-57]

~

Give courtesy and kindness with love to your family, for the visit is short and the parting merely waits.   [2-23-59]

~

The influence of the strength of a united family has no boundaries, lasts for decades, and has a cycle.   [9-2-80]

FATHERS

When a young man fathers a child, aid him well for you aid not one but three.   [10-3-81]

FAULTLESSNESS

This you cannot have, faultlessness; none shall be perfect, and this too is for the good of each, and that love may be—and a line of the pattern shows.   [4-18-63]

FAULTS

Salt and faults be the same, and can aid or not.   [7-15-58]

~

Accuse a man of small faults, and you praise him.[7-23-58]

~

A picker of berries gains a little and a scratched hand; and a fault finder gains naught and a bad bruise.   [4-1-59]

~

Repair your faults as you can, as this gives a better choice of friends.   [5-23-59]

~

It requires a blow to crack an egg, you must dig to have a cellar; and to cure a fault requires more than a blow and a dig.   [4-1-61]

~

Keep a sharp lookout for a nugget in a river bed; keep a sharp lookout for an arrow that might come from an ambush; but keep not a sharp lookout for a fault in another, for this is small and passes quickly.   [10-14-61]

~

Small faults are as a dagger's point.   [10-7-63]

~

One with many faults has no friends, and it is so with a man who has too few faults; and it is so with the man who has a few certain faults.   [2-20-65]

FAVORED
The favored receive as a gentle shower and as the softness of dew.   [5-27-55]

~

If one refuses you a favor, anger not, for he is a fool or has a reason.   [3-14-61]

FEARS
You may not fear more than you may.   [1-9-57]

~

You shall shed your fears as a snake sheds its skin, save one; and it grows and grows and becomes no longer a fear.

[5-16-60]

~

There are but two fears: the fear of a howling, growling, prowling wolf pack, and the fear that a great chasm may come under an ocean so that the heat of the Earth's core will bring hot steam and you cannot find seed.   [10-13-64]

FEEDING

Feed a horse well and he serves better; and your body is better than a horse.   [8-13-58]

FIGHTING

Be you one or many, you need not fight; and a fight, like a fig bush, needs cultivating.   [4-29-59]

FINDING

Finding a diamond brings cutting and polishing; finding laborers sitting under a tree brings a search for profitable use of their skills, and is better than finding a diamond.   [4-11-62]

~

A dog barks at the moon and knows not to find iron and copper; and a man finding iron and copper is not as a dog barking at the moon.   [4-13-62]

~

A woman finds all from her child; a man loses most when he loses his health.   [10-3-63]

FINISHING

The planets are there—the oceans are contained; but the Earth is not yet a garden and the things unfinished need listing and study.   [6-10-59]

FIRE

A fire burns, warms, cooks, so go forth knowing. [9-25-57]

FOOD

Take no more than a fair portion of the food for it becomes as a poison and a waste.   [8-17-56]

~

The methods of food distribution to all are simple and involved; and the people learn where the spring comes forth.   [9-6-56]

~

The effects of the necessity of eating control and govern all; but a horse is best guided by two reins.   [9-11-56]

~

The air shows an even distribution for all to breathe, though storms come; and it is the same with food.   [3-15-60]

FOOLS

You must flee from two fools gathered together.

If there be more than two you have a riot, and if a demogogue obtains control of your country, he will seize your home, give it to others, and send you off to war.   [1-26-78]

FOOLISHNESS

A dog barking in the night is heard afar; and a shining light is seen; and as you speak, your foolishness is as the barking dog and a shining light.   [10-29-61]

FORCE

Force begetteth little and meets a sharp edge.   [9-25-57]

FORGETFULNESS

Forgetfulness is one of the blessings; and in it you can find peace and daily laughter.   [9-6-56]

FORGIVENESS
A great river begins, travels over rapids, merges into the sea and is gone; but it has served well, and forgiveness is the same.   [11-3-59]

~

Judge and forgive thyself, for this you alone can do, and thus relieve the burn of regrets.   [7-15-78]

FORNICATION
Fornicate not for this builds a stinking memory and you cannot dam the injury.   [12-23-64]

FREEDOM
There be many freedoms and a man can delve into all structures, even create a new thing, and this is great.   [5-15-59]

~

Break a rock, chisel and polish, and it will help make a garden; and you are free to do this.   [10-25-60]

FRIENDSHIP
Laugh aloud among friends, and cry alone that few may hear.   [8-10-56]

~

Test not thy friends lest it be as a dropped egg.   [12-4-56]

~

An unjust attack is best defended by your friends, even unto your farthest neighbor.   [6-6-57]

~

Invoke not a just attack, lest thy friends be embarrassed and depart.   [6-6-57]

~

Let love delude, 'tis well; fear fear, it destroys but may aid you; receive courage from a friend, build it, share it, though some who are born with it be fools.   [6-19-57]

~

You are given air to breath all your days, friendship you get by first giving—the love in your family must be nurtured hourly.   [6-26-57]

~

There is little that costs more and is worth less than bad companions.   [7-6-57]

~

Your friends can harm you, your friends can aid you, and of the two, the first will surprise you.   [7-12-57]

~

Consider your surroundings, and regard your friends, for you cannot do otherwise.   [10-29-57]

~

And a lion eat your friend, kill the lion; and it helps not your friend, but the world is better for men.   [4-2-58]

~

Pull a feather and a bird squawks; and a friend breaks an arm and you are slowed.   [8-19-58]

~

Build a door that keepeth out the rain and lets your friends enter; and if it be not squared exactly, yet it serves well.   [8-19-58]

~

A broken limb falls from a tree to the ground and leaves a scar; a friend departs from thee and this leaves a scar that outlasts the tree.   [11-27-59]

~

The glow of twilight is as the friendships of your father who has passed on.   [12-11-61]

~

If you seek friends without fault, you will go a lonely road for days without end.   [12-21-61]

~

Cast away thy riches, yea, cast into a river a great diamond of world renown for its luster before you cast away a friend, for he who casts away a friend stands bare.   [8-15-74]

FUTURE

In the next 500 years: Space travel is sure. One people, one race (with exceptional minorities). Controlled money, of constant value as on a measuring rod. Longer life. One government—freedom of travel—better homes, food and this and that.   [6-28-56]

~

Salutations to the men to be, when time and hunger no longer stalk the land.   [9-13-56]

~

Improve that which is here that men may have greater beauty and do better, for therein lies great gain.   [4-11-57]

~

Plan, all men, plan together, plan your path and deeds.   [5-8-57]

~

By the year 2250: a commonly used language both taught and prescribed; a working world government abolishing, practically, war. Likely a republic, using a one-money system, freedom of travel, and right of ownership of property.

By the year of 2500, the loss of racial differences and the emergence of a composite, but still not fully complete.   [1-10-75]

GAMBLING

The man who casts his money in gambles at high odds for progress deserves a salute.   [3-11-57]

GENERATIONS

That generation which builds with its labor and materials that which later generations may freely have, loses nothing and has peace.   [7-18-60]

~

A drop of water falls into the ocean and is gone, but the water remains risen—a man ate an apple a thousand years ago, and both are gone, but we are better from them; so shoe thy feet with good shoes and do what you do well, for generations to come depend thereon.   [12-23-64]

GENEROSITY

Generosity is best measured by the cost to the giver.   [4-21-78]

GIFTS

If another forces a small gift upon thee, take it and smile, and he has had his reward.   [9-21-63]

GIVING

Beware of the unselfish, lest you overgive them.   [10-4-56]

~

Brides and leadership may be seized, but both must be served.   [12-4-56]

~

Aid the strong for you share their victories.   [2-16-57]

~

Refresh the man who exhausts his strength in harnessing the forces of nature, even though he do it for himself, which he cannot.   [3-11-57]

~

Aid and merchandise bought by money are not bad, and will ring sound.   [5-18-57]

~

Neighbors will first give aid and friendship; but afterwards they must be daily earned.   [5-18-57]

~

A small present is a gracious thing and best repaid with a smile.   [6-8-57]

~

Demand not of a giving hand, for it dryeth it, and turns it into a fire, even thy parents'.   [8-20-57]

He who is given a stone wall has not placed the stones therein, and knoweth not their roundness.   [8-20-57]

~

Give, and you increase; keep and you lessen.   [12-31-57]

~

Give, and be known not, and this tripleth the sure return.
                                                        [12-31-57]

~

A stranger giveth a gift and shall receive a sharp look.
                                                        [2-25-58]

~

You have that which you earn and that which is given and that which is given is half as good.   [6-19-58]

~

And you have a thousand loaves, you can give to the needy; and you have two thousand loaves, the greedy and lazy will find you; and you have a third thousand loaves, the greedy and lazy will contend that you owe them and say, "Did we not wait while you baked"; so giving is acid that cuts away a false covering.   [9-4-58]

~

Give your baby strong wine, and your friends credit, when the need arises.   [10-17-58]

~

A stick has two points, and these are not equal; and a giver of gifts measures the costs, and the receiver looks at the worth, and neither is right.   [11-5-59]

~

A wooden bridge has planks and nails, and each nail requires a hammerblow; and as you live, if you give a hammerblow and another gives a plank, the plank giver may have done better, though proof there is not.   [9-4-61]

~

To grab a tiger's tail brings little profit; and to give a gift for profit is less worthy than grabbing a tiger's tail.   [5-15-62]

~

If you receive much property and monies, and defeat the tax collectors and embezzlers, then you must pass the Golden Test, lest you prove yourself unwise in giving.   [8-19-75]

~

The pleasure of giving exceeds the flavor of the fresh fruits of the new season.   [5-4-82]

GLORIES

There be two glories that exceed sweet clover—the strength of the young man and the beauty of the young woman.   [10-16-63]

GOD

And the year two thousand shall pass, and yet another three score and ten, and on the following day at high noon on the Earth's highest peak, let a note be sounded on a golden triangle, each side of a full twelve inches and of the weight of twelve ounces; and let the hammer be of silver and of one twelfth of the weight of one side. Have all instruments in readiness that the note be carried afar that all may hear who will hear.

At the sound of the note, be quiet, raise your hands for the thought "we pray that our God return to this earth, that all men may see."

Having so done, depart. On the next day and hour, at the sound of the triangle bring your most beloved, to such a place as you have chosen, and kneel and raise your hands fully, and be silent, and think again; and depart.

And on the third day and hour, at the sound of the triangle, let all who will, joined by all who will, at their chosen place, kneel, raise your hands, speak clearly and say, "Our God who gave us life and being, return openly to Earth and forgive our weaknesses and guide us forever." And depart, and if God heed thee not, so be it!

Let an unbeliever strike the triangle, that all others may have a part.   [2-14-58]

GOODNESS
Knoweth the good, seek the good, learn the good, that you may truly be and not idly cry in the sun.   [9-20-57]
~

The good receive the good, and the disobedient be failed again and again and daily and continually, and at the end an eraser cometh forth and they are forgotten.   [9-20-57]
~

Goodness sheddeth a light, a bright light, and it cannot be covered and needs no mirror.   [10-31-57]
~

The good deeds of others cast a soft glow upon the road that you may better see.   [4-29-60]
~

You can sin, in limits; and you can harm in limits and the good you can do is unlimited and this persisteth.   [12-12-60]
~

The good lasts long; and the bad goes as the dirt from a washed cloak.   [6-8-62]
~

The cost of doing good is small and easily borne. [10-6-64]

GOSSIP
Approach not a spouting volcano and a talking gossip, stand back and far.   [12-29-58]

GRATITUDE
Let your gratitude be not like a puff of smoke in the air.   [6-19-58]
~

Gratitude gives a light as of a thousand candles. [11-18-59]

~

Someone gave fire, another the wheel, some nations honor, and you cannot give them gratitude.   [2-13-63]

~

It shines in the grass, it shines so brightly in the sky that the stars are dimmed, and men live their best when they live in the golden beams that come from that which is called gratitude.
[8-25-74]

GRAVITY

Gravity serves as does the least of things; so a question, "Whence have you immunity if you crush a fly?"   [8-1-61]

GREATNESS

A man grows wheat, and creates; and another quiets quarrelling men, and brings peace; and neither is greater for the eye cannot hear.   [11-19-58]

~

Clench you fist in the air, and open it, and you have a hole; clench you fist and sink it into the ocean and draw it forth, and there is a hole; and these holes are greater than is left when the greatest of men passes.   [12-31-59]

GUESSING

An arrow shot in the dark strikes a deer, and the deer runs away, and is lost; and a wild guess may wreck a great ship.
[2-8-58]

GUIDANCE

All are guided by needs, wants and wishes.   [5-20-55]

HABIT

Habit is a strong cord, and wrap it not around your throat, lest it choke you.   [5-5-58]

HAPPINESS

Happiness is sweet to the troubled.   [2-6-56]

~

Happiness flees with satisfaction of desires.   [3-26-56]

~

Forget and forgive pull the chariot of happiness over hills, it moves not without them.   [8-27-57]

~

Each shall have happiness in full, to have and to be lost, for it comes as the rising of great waters; and unhappiness is measured finely.   [2-23-62]

~

Happiness shines as a great candle, and it needs a roof, it is best fueled by the produce of the fields, and its light streams forth through the window and all the neighbors and strangers are pleasured.   [3-8-62]

~

The happiness of a stranger is more important than a day's labor.   [4-15-62]

~

You know happiness from unhappiness—that which is good for thy body and that which is not—but you cannot tell the difference from thy troubles and the troubles of others.
[9-15-64]

~

As you rise each day, build happiness inside, greet all with a smile, and you will have many rewards.   [10-8-79]

HARSH WORDS

Rain falls upon a roof, pattereth, and runneth off; a little axe chops a tree, it falls; an avalanche makes loud noises and stops;

but a harsh word liveth on and on, until there is a flood of forgiveness, which must come from another.   [4-16-58]

HATE

Hate cannot be bought—it is given or earned.   [6-23-57]

~

Hateth not this and that, even the cold eye of a shark.
[11-15-57]

~

The preachers of hate and vengeance occupy at least two bad places:

(a) in the area of economic struggle for bread and water, as their profits rarely outlast the morning dew; and

(b) in happiness, for they have many fears and bad dreams and cannot sleep well.   [10-8-79]

HAVING

Those who have do readily ask much of those who have.
[10-19-56]

~

One has not that which he holds; he is not what he hopes to be; and he is not where he will be.   [5-19-60]

~

Ten thousand things you may have to serve you; but take care lest you serve the ten thousand things.   [5-28-60]

~

Many live in high places, in low places, in hot places, and cold; and none have equal measures of food, and yet none have not.   [9-13-60]

~

A man who has but a crust of bread, has not much; a man with good land, a home and many sheep for clothing, without a heavy crown to wear, has much.   [9-2-64]

HEALTH
Chain a large rock to your arm with a barbed chain and this you can carry; but add not fat to your body for this you cannot.
[10-30-58]

HELPING
He who aids the unsavory earns a double ribbon and must wash his hands.
[12-30-57]

~

A coin has two sides; and so it is with a cripple, who, stumbling, receives a helping hand, and yet the cripple must not use the path of the speeding chariot.
[1-12-59]

HISTORY
History records those who have done good to many evil ones, or done evil to many good ones, or came close to giving the difference between good and evil.
[1-19-78]

~

A shortage of pure water, a steady population level, and a lacing of paved roads marks the end of the investment phase of this continent.
[11-2-78]

HONESTY
Cherish your honesty for it is a gift, and cometh of old and continueth on.
[10-29-57]

~

Four ounces of beans are worth more than one ounce, all say; but to a man with a ton of beans, it is not so; yet who can say an honest act is worth more than a cheery word? [2-5-59]

~

An honest man's mistakes grow as trees in the forest; let not a dishonest man call his act a green tree.
[5-20-59]

If the beggar shame thee for passing, he is not truly a beggar;
and he who parades his poverty has time for other things.
[12-19-60]

HONOR
Look around and you will see fervor among the ministering
and the protesting, for they thus seek honor.   [8-17-56]

~

Respect and honor any man, for he seeks these as part of his
recompense.   [3-11-57]

~

Tear a man's honor away and you bruise his soul.
[10-15-57]

HUMAN RACE
A wagon that sticketh in the road needs a shove and the
driver pays a coin; to cast rocks in the road brings a lash from
the whip; and the human race seems as a wagon, and you can
know if you shove or cast rocks.   [5-20-60]

HUNTING
The hunt for the better way, the better thing, is pressed
mightily this August 1960; and the reward is much greater than
a piece of meat and a hairy hide.   [8-11-60]

~

One hunter brings a deer and another may bring a rabbit,
and there is a difference as twigs upon a tree.   [10-31-61]

~

Man has hunted the beasts of the field, and few are left; he
has hunted the germs of the air and is gaining a victory; and
sought wisdom but here he finds a spectrum and is yet awed.
[12-29-61]

IDEAS
A beautiful rose pleases the eye, a mine brings riches, but an idea is a golden light that brightens the far mountains.

[1-16-60]

IDLENESS
Burn your shocked wheat, cast your oxen over a cliff, but idle not a day away, saving the Seventh.   [8-6-58]

~

A three-pronged fork has three prongs, and none sound as the others when struck, so it is with idleness, laziness and resting.   [9-14-58]

~

Beware of idle reading for it steals the hours away. [6-2-78]

IGNORANCE
Struggle not against the bonds cast by ignorance—struggle against ignorance.   [9-5-62]

~

A volcano casts a pall of ashes and lava; but the pall cast by ignorance is deeper, lasts longer and hurts worse.   [6-1-64]

IMPATIENCE
Impatience burneth thee with a bad burn.   [9-13-63]

IMPERFECTION
A fruit is perfectly wrapped, a butterfly's wings have sure coloring and design, and imperfection lieth not with such as these.   [1-7-60]

INJURIES
Your injuries come of an accident, less than a fourth; from the intent of another, less than a tenth; and of foolishness.

[6-4-59]

INJUSTICE

A widow cried out, "Jones is a thief," and all the neighbors heard, and it was false; and he had no ear to hear, but he was sheltered and did not suffer, thus ending the search for injustice.   [6-11-60]

INTELLIGENCE

Only untrammeled human intelligence can cope with the situation.   [3-14-79]

~

Only human intelligence can evaluate human intelligence, which as yet cannot be done.   [3-14-79]

INSTRUCTION

Pour not water on a turtle's back, and give not instructions to one who asks it not.   [12-11-61]

JEALOUSY

Jealousy burns its bearer; and like a hot flame dies soon, or turns to hate.   [7-24-57]

JOURNEYS

If you journey, first climb a high hill, eat of your food and look ahead, and thus find the game trails and water.
                    [3-29-59]

~

If you journey for two days, carry enough for three days, but if you carry enough for five days you will have a three-day journey.   [9-22-63]

JOY

Share your joy, 'tis best, and your pain, for none does better by their keeping.   [8-10-56]

~

Build joy and pleasure carefully as sorrow is a close sister.
[11-14-57]

~

Joy and happiness are as a fruit on a tree, and are not lost as a leaf in wintry blasts; and are as drops of water in a brook that goes into a lake and all may dip therein.   [11-3-63]

~

Share thy joy and victories with thy neighbor, for he fully shares your ills.   [12-19-63]

~

The sources of joy are not unlimited; but may be most productive by care and planning; and best used by the moderate.   [11-23-74]

JUDGMENT
All have limited experience and judgment, and he who expresses an opinion and leadership, by this alone betrays bad judgment.   [12-21-56]

~

Trust your own judgment and experience, as you must; and trust the judgment of others later.   [12-21-56]

~

He who gives a sharp judgment clashes swords.   [9-11-58]

~

There is a whence and why of thieves and liars and such ilk, of which there is always plenty; and they be judged and have vengeance and their judges are judged.   [11-27-62]

~

If you would be as a dog that chases its tail, appraise thyself.
[9-23-63]

JUSTICE
The just are compensated more fully, more lastingly, and most slowly that it be fully earned.   [4-20-57]

~

Justice comes of courts, which is not the best; and from neighbors, which is better; and from above which leadeth no further.   [1-29-59]

~

Two plus two is four and this has not changed and can be written and is steady; but the justness of the pay of the worker for his labor is far more steady.   [1-19-60]

KINDNESS

Be kind to the mean and wicked as they have themselves as their enemy; and kindness is as warm soup.   [12-4-56]

KNOWLEDGE

You may know that which you know.   [4-30-57]

~

You can be drawn to knowledge, knowledge can be poured upon you, but a stone turns cold again.   [8-20-57]

~

And the question, "You know these, and how do you?" and the answer is, "I know not—nor why."   [11-25-57]

~

The bed of a river is bare, there being no water; and the field is dusty, it being rocky; and a man without knowledge is an empty dish.   [5-1-58]

~

Step not on the foot of another and this you know, and do not; and so you are what you know.   [6-5-58]

~

You know the hiss of the snake, the growl of a dog and other things, and know them well for they come straight and from afar, and there is an afar.   [6-10-58]

~

Run a run, walk a walk, play a part and know this for you do better.   [7-25-58]

~

There is the night, then comes the dawn, then the day; and a man is seen, he speaks, and he does and you so know him. [7-30-58]

~

Set not a rock hen on an egg, as the egg will sour; put not an unknowing man on rich land, as he is a rock hen. [10-14-58]

~

The tide runs freely, and the father trains his son; and the tide turns, and the son learneth more, and speaks up. [10-25-58]

~

A dog barks in a cave, and you know it is a dog; a woman sings in a house, and it is a woman in happiness; and so it is with that which lives within you; as you speak, so it is known. [1-2-59]

~

There are some things that all know; some things not observed by all; and some things unknown to all. [5-4-59]

~

Knowledge is peculiar in volume, it must be stored in books; some remains unchanged and pure; some becomes squared and will not fit; and every time it is used, it must be reexamined. [1-29-60]

~

Break not your jug carelessly, and this you know, and this you learn. [4-11-61]

~

A peacock is known when he spreads his feathers so richly colored; and a man is known more ways than there are feathers in a peacock's tail. [11-21-61]

~

Let each man know his own hunger and feed himself; none can do it better. [3-29-63]

~

There is a great fount of knowledge in the distance; and our brains are lighted as a candle. [12-4-64]

~

All know to breathe, every boy knows to run and play; and a list of such would make for a surer knowledge sooner. [12-6-64]

~

Put thy knowledge in a book, its memory fadeth not, and is ever ready and fresh for a seeker.   [3-3-75]

~

When a man walks forth from the shadow cast by the tree of ignorance into some newfound light cast by the star of knowledge, all else pauses and waits in due deference to the creator to see what shall be made new.   [9-19-78]

~

Again—use all knowledge and wisdom in the selection of the food for your body, for there is no better use of them.

[1-21-80]

LABOR

Stalks of grain are leveled; and the labor of all is leveled.
[4-18-60]

~

Take from a man his necessity for labor, and you take the sweetness from his honey.   [5-1-60]

~

What remains from the labor of billions—what remains from the labor of this year—what will remain after the passage of five thousand years of labor—this causes a great book.
[5-17-61]

~

The morning dew and chance to labor last not past the day.
[6-6-63]

~

Of those who labor, the carpenter hangs the door upon the house, and this is used each day.   [7-31-64]

~

Heirs and a few others need not labor, and their cake fattens and palls, and their bread is rarely hot.   [6-28-65]

LABORER
A laborer hungers not; and his dirty hands pride him much.   [10-26-61]

LACKING
There are two lacks—the lack of information and true knowledge.   [7-28-61

LAND
Land was open; land was settled and worked and held; land is taken and blocked, and this will not endure.   [1-27-60]

LAUGHTER
Seek moments of laughter, for they have much in common with drops of dew.   [7-27-57]

~

Laugh and pray and make cheerful noises, live and love, and these you may do, and they have no set value.   [11-7-57]

~

A struck anvil gives a tone, and it varies not; but its constancy is small as compared to the laughter of playing men.   [11-28-58]

~

A frog croaks, a dog barks at a shadow, and a man laughs loudly, and of the three the laugh pleases most, but just a little.   [5-20-63]

~

Laughter marks a carefree moment.   [3-20-80]

LAWS
The laws of chance, of nature, of the universe are sure; the laws of men wobble.   [5-28-57]

~

The error of the courts of men sting, and having stung, quite often cure.   [6-26-57]

~

A witness who tells the truth is a good witness, and a deceiver stinks.   [6-29-57]

~

Also it behooves you to observe the laws passed by men.   [10-30-58]

~

The lawmakers make laws under other laws not written.   [5-7-80]

LEADERSHIP

You who lead must lead and eternally be moving—there is no stopping for the leader.   [5-31-57]

~

The smart ones maketh the leader who has pains; and they have as much and hide behind a curtain.   [9-3-57]

LEARNING

The sun and learning maketh easier walking.   [1-18-58]

~

The seas hold more water than you can drink, though but a swallow; the sky holds air, but a breath; and so, pick what you would learn, for you must.   [12-10-58]

~

A tail can be cut from a cat, and the cat is not the same; let not learning cut off a part of thee.   [5-18-59]

~

A baby knows the suck; a boy learns of the ball; a man learns to trade grain and of a family; then he feels the warmth of the sun, feels the solidity of the Earth and ponders on the fact that these were not made by men, and so reaches a turn in a path of learning.   [6-5-61]

LEISURE
Use rest, consume pleasure, for these are compensations.
[8-3-56]

~

Leisure is a reward for work well done.   [3-20-80]

LENDING
You may give, sell, lose, die and lend; and of these be a quick lender for you both have and two have the use of it. [4-15-62]

LIARS
Liars, thieves and gossips may abuse you, and your friends draw aside; but go the high and lonely road, yield not, and this makes you better.   [8-29-61]

LIES
Spew bubbles in the air, for this is of more use than defending yourself against false charges.   [4-23-60]

~

Let not a poisonous reptile pass, yet much greater damage arises from an unchallenged lie.   [12-14-64]

LIFE
To live gives the right to have what is needed.   [10-6-55]

~

Live and resurrect for good, punishment and reward.
[5-15-58]

~

A razor's edge is sharp and serves, much wheat is grown that bread may rise, and men live and do more than breathe.
[11-11-58]

~

Ask yourself "do I want to live forever" not "must I too die," though each has a common answer, for solace comes from the first.   [2-5-60]

~

Centuries ago long life was tried and abandoned, then the rule of three score and ten came; and now it seems that this too is passing.   [8-22-60]

~

A leaf drifts on the current of a brook and one can see the direction of the flow—on the seashore the tide comes and goes, and you know this has been done before; and as life on the Earth lives one can see the direction it moves, and can know this too has been done before.   [9-21-74]

~

A blue vista and you can see far from the pinnacle of your life, a peak that passes easily and is unknown.   [3-17-75]

~

An imbalance of life has resulted from the escape by men from a law of life, "Eat and be eaten."   [6-25-78]

~

During the past thousand years the proliferation of human life has been a great event; and the ability of the many segments to breed gives rise to a great question.   [8-26-78]

LIGHT

Lightning striketh here and there, and fame too—he who has fame has a mole on his back—who chooseth a grain of wheat over a loaf of bread?   [8-27-57]

~

You walk, talk, eat, breathe and need light, and you shall have light and need not walk, talk, eat, and breathe.[6-19-58]

~

Pause not if you have a good candle and obtain a lamp; set the candle aside, the lamp serves better.   [4-14-60]

~

A wild flame in a forest glows brightly as night falls; and the hairs of your head give a brighter light than the wild flame that you may more clearly understand.   [10-28-63]

LIKING

To like another is a fair wind and you may sail with it; dislike is a secret snake, stone it. [8-28-57]

LIST

The list "we have" lengthens; the list "we have not" has long ago come to one, and even this may give way to the hands of man. [8-5-60]

LISTENING

If a rock falls, it makes a thud; and if a man speaks, listen, for it is not as the thud of the falling rock. [4-11-60]

~

Listen and learn, that you bruise not nor plant thy seed on stony ground, and lose thy seed; listen and learn, for this is best. [2-5-64]

LIVING

Each must seek his own best life, though one's best may be another's regret. [9-11-56]

~

The price of living is within the bounds of each. [10-15-56]

~

If you ask, "Why do I live this day?" an answer: you live this day that you may do that which you do this day; and fear not the morrow. [12-14-62]

LONELINESS

You go not alone, nor can you for long; and the sun shines for the many. [6-8-62]

~

Among the lonely is found the traveller and his clothes are dirty. [1-25-65]

LOSS

To lose is to first have, and it lasteth a while.   [11-7-57]

~

Spill soup on your raiment, and this is loss; a thief steals a ruby, and this is loss; but when all is taken, this is not loss.
[1-23-58]

~

Take a doll from a baby, and the baby has a loss; and if your house is lost, your loss is as the loss of the doll.
[5-18-59]

~

An egg dropped and broken soaks into the ground and is lost; but this is not so with men now, has been not so in the past; and the why needs nursing.   [9-22-59]

~

Ghenghis Khan, Attilla and Hitler danced, and the losses were great; but the loss from an idea abandoned and undone exceedeth these—now and in the time to be, wealth and good is found in ideas, used and done.   [2-4-64]

LOVE

A woman's soul is molded by those she loves.   [4-20-57]

~

You and a brick wall can be broken and repaired; but love and fine crystal must be handled gently.   [7-2-57]

~

Love and happiness are as great oceans with enough for all that have been, that are, and shall be; and those that have been are as a mustard seed.   [5-26-59]

~

A tree will lose its leaves, and you shall have losses, and your losses shall be as the falling leaves.   [4-29-60]

~

Light goeth through a carrier in space—all beings, man and

animal, find a common greeting everywhere, and this is sometimes called love.   [1-16-56, revised 8-25-65]

~

Love comes from the light of the Sun; and lasts longer than
the light of the day.   [9-11-81]

~

Margaret

A wire of steel can bind thee—the web of a spider hinders not
the smallest move; and the bonds of love compare to the wire of
steel, as the wire of steel compares to the web of the spider.
[9-11-81]

LUXURY

Seek not luxury in rich cakes, silken drapes and royal
coaches; but in charity.   [11-17-61]

LYING

He who lies, walks alone.   [2-26-57]

~

One may lie in many ways, but all are in vain.   [2-26-57]

MADNESS

Beware of him who cries "strike him" for he is as mad as a
dog that foams at the mouth.   [1-16-60]

MAN

Man can see mankind with the eyes of man only. [7-16-55]

~

A feather grows upon a hen and each is new and separate;
and so is man, but who can say a man is less than a chicken
feather?   [12-12-56]

~

The ultimate purpose of men has not been served, though
seventy times seven thousand decades may have passed, the
vista broadens as our eyes open.   [3-11-57]

~

A little, and a bad man is made; but a good man is builded through the years. [7-6-57]

~

There is a composite this day, and all there is is there, and man has his part. [8-13-58]

~

A pool lies quietly in the sun until a breeze comes; and men's affairs lie like a pool and need a breeze. [1-28-59]

~

Mortar in a wall serves, a river drains waste water; but man seemeth a user. [4-23-59]

~

An inch is an inch, and is known; a dog is a dog and this sufficeth; but truly a man is neither an inch nor a dog. [10-27-59]

~

Many figures are required to measure the smallness of things in relation to the size of man—many figures are required to measure the largeness of things in relation to man; and if man varies his size, many circumstances will be altered. [11-22-74]

MARTYRDOM

Do not be a martyr uncalled, lest you burn uselessly and unwanted. [12-6-56]

MEANING

The word water has one meaning; the word forgiveness has as many as there are men; yet one cannot live without water, nor live fully without forgiveness. [4-11-63]

MEANNESS

To have another do your meanness is to compound the folly; and to do another's meanness is to be a fool's fool. [5-27-55]

MEASUREMENT

Count the grains of sand on the beach and in the deserts; weigh the rocks in the mountains, and bit by bit; and number the mountains, and on the south of each dig a protective cave, and place a book therein that men write what they find.
[4-12-58]

~

Measure your gold to a split ounce, for you will anyway, and measure your strength and time more so, for surely your heirs will find your gold in a cave.
[4-12-58]

~

Take a pound of lead in your hand and this seems not much; t.ke a pound of hair, and this seemeth more; and a thief steal your raiment, and a guard steals your gold, and yet a thief is but a thief, and a pound is but a pound.
[4-14-58]

~

A pound of beans is worth more than a half pound or an ounce; and if you have an appointment it is better to be ahead than on time or late.
[7-30-58]

~

For, strange as it seems, you may measure the labor that you do.
[7-1-61]

~

A man has many successes and a few mistakes, yet he is best measured by his mistakes and his successes, not by either alone.
[1-20-65]

MEMORY

Memory is a written slate for reading.
[5-15-57]

~

Parings from toenails, the fruit of yesterday, that which you now have, that which you have tomorrow build memories, and these alone you can keep.
[7-22-61]

A needle remains a needle and forgets not what it does, and the same with a hammer; and this memory of things never fails.
[8-13-64]

MEN

Men of strong minds and bodies and beautiful women breathe deeply of the cool air of the mountains and eat of the fruit of the valley; and the women are given this by these men; and these men take as a matter of right.   [1-13-64]

~

There is that from which the grains of the fields are made, and it is limited; and the grains of the fields are made into men, and these are unnumbered.   [10-15-64]

MIND

He who cultivates a fertile valley increases its yield; and he who cultivates his mind finds it as a fertile valley.   [1-19-60]

MIRACLES

Miracles bring great fear and a spirit of futility.   [9-15-56]

MISERY

All is brighter to those emerging from the dark, and your miseries are as the dark.   [2-6-56]

~

Search for misery and pain, and it is a long search; and what you find is soon eased and over-cured.   [1-4-60]

MISTAKES

A mistake needs considering, amend fully at once, and do it not again, unless a dolt.   [7-24-57]

~

Angels' mistakes cannot be cured by men, nor noted, nor done.   [8-27-57]

~

Mistakes be of two kinds, thine and another's; and of these chagrin becometh thee and a smile oileth the other.

[10-30-57]

MONEY

A swirling wind picks the sand from the desert and loses it; and the money you have is no more than the desert sand, and has been swirled many times; and yet is as the fresh fruit from the tree.   [7-27-60]

~

A handful of snow and easy money are hard to hold.

[7-10-63]

MOTHER

Never wrong, always of great gain—a mother feeds her child, a man builds a home.   [9-18-62]

MOURNING

A great tree falls before repeated axe strokes, and mourning goes as the days pass.   [7-24-59]

MOVEMENT

The galaxies move in greatness, the storm tosses waves, and a ridden horse travels a high trail; and all these are movement and merit thought.   [10-18-62]

MURDERER

A murderer hath two ears on his head, and these a prison make.   [5-24-63]

MUSIC

A golden throne giveth a glow and a hard seat; he who sitteth under a grapevine may feed a bird and hear sweet music.

[7-1-58]

NATIONS

Rain falls a drop at a time, and forms a great river that is controlled by its banks; and all are born one at a time, and form great nations and have their controls too.   [7-29-59]

NATURE

A pink cloud shows the coming dawn, and look around you as the clouds are .pink.   [10-3-60]

~

The grass turned the land green; and the forest turned the land green and the grass passed; and came men and the land had homes and was green, and the forest passed, and this is not the end of this.   [12-24-63]

NECESSITY

It may be—That you must fall upon a bush of thorns—
That you must go among vipers with fangs bared—
That you must put your body in flames—
But you must not kill yourself.   [1-29-59]

~

Necessity brings forth loved ones; needs are best served by friends; wants bring enemies.   [11-27-59]

NEED

You need, and you need much, and on and on except what you must have and this comes quickly, minute by minute.   [12-5-57]

~

You that have salute those that travel empty-handed, for their smile arises from the exercise of courage, or is a plea for aid.   [4-30-57]

~

Drink not of scummy water and alcohol, and eat not of the swill of hogs, you need not.   [1-13-58]

~

Climb the mountains though the rich ores are gone, for new needs and new knowledge bring a searching light—climb the mountains. [12-14-64]

NEIGHBORS
Neighbors aid the parents in the care of their child, and the parents of the child and others gain rewards. [2-28-78]

NEW
The search for the new began in the beginning, continues now, and numbers fail to provide a day when the search ends. [5-3-78]

NEWNESS
Experimentation is plain to see in the new. [9-20-55]

~

All progress is first wrapped in newness; and also is green fruit. [12-20-56]

~

Something new, something new, something new for everyone each day—try the new, try the new, try the new.
[12-20-56]

~

Chop the trees and bushes with a new axe, and the olden trail will carry you safely. [3-8-58]

NOISE
Volcanoes give forth loud noises, violence, and bad gas; and anger too, and these are the good things. [11-18-57]

OLD AGE
Hide behind a tree, dig a hole and place a large rock over it, if you must flee; but if you flee from old age or illness, you can find no place to hide. [9-23-74]

OPTIMISM

Paint your carriage in bright colors that you may ride in style, grease well the wheels of your wagon that it may carry its load; keep the corners of your mouth up and your shoulders squared for this maketh thee as a brightly colored carriage and a well-greased wagon.   [9-8-61]

ORIGINS

Sit upon a porch, rest your feet on a rail and ask yourself, "How came I here?" Go back not past the age of six, and if you seem floating jetsam carried by currents and vagrant winds, know that this is not so as you merely know not.   [7-1-61]

OTHERS

You cannot step in another's tracks, for your toes be larger or smaller and not his nor shall be.   [12-5-57]

~

Hurl not a knife into another, for surely there is no gain and you place your own head on a block.   [12-19-57]

~

Fie not the world for this gets laughter; fie not your neighbors for this makes you walk alone; fie not a friend for this is disaster; fie not your family nor any member, for this you must not do.   [8-26-58]

~

Chop off the hand of another and you cannot return it; block another's path and you take his time and cannot return it.

[8-28-58]

~

A scorpion appears, stamp it with a well-shod foot; a tiger growls, kill it with a long spear; and you need food, kill it; but another is not a scorpion, tiger or food.   [2-27-59]

~

You are not today as you were yesterday, nor will be tomorrow as today; so are all others, and you must learn anew today the man you knew yesterday, and you shall not know him tomorrow as today.   [3-9-59]

~

Consider that which causes you to like another, dislike another or pass him as a face in the crowd, as to whether it is action or words or both, and this is old.   [9-28-60]

OWNING

A man owns his home and it is a crime for a burglar, tax collector or invader to break his door; and all know this, among other things.   [3-5-65]

PAIN

Pain and fear are servants, and these best serve when understood.   [2-6-62]

PAINTING

A painter paints a picture, and surely you are more than a daub of paint, though you last not as long.   [4-11-61]

PARADOX

A paradox—each must drink his water, each must walk alone; yet is well known that each is part of one and the entity is part of each.   [3-17-75]

PARENTS

This happens for certain, and is true, all parents eat the better.   [11-18-57]

PARTS

These be parts: Food, clothing, transportation and entertainment; and these have many parts, and the many parts can be improved.   [10-28-63]

PASSING

The informed, he who knows much, thinketh upon his passing, for pass he will, and he will care if his passing be deemed good or bad, or be good or bad or neither.   [12-5-57]

PASSION

A man howls, he grovels, he has no dignity, he has his greatest burden in his passion.   [4-3-64]

PAST

That that is gone is well gone; and that that is to come is better.   [3-17-58]

~

The past is marked for mapping; and the best is not wars, kings and boundaries.   [8-13-59]

~

The past remains close, so very close; and things go tumbling in, yet a few things stay out and with one, so very few.

[11-3-81]

PATTERNS

Pick a berry from a bush, and it is like no other berry, and this shows a sure line of a full pattern.   [1-6-60]

~

All are not the same, even one to another, nor have been, and this seems a line of the pattern.   [12-29-60]

~

Plant a peach seed and cometh a peach tree and a line in the great pattern appears; and to trace a line, consider a boy who becometh a man, but you know not his fruit.   [3-27-62]

PEACE

You shall see a stranger lost in wild waters, and you see: then a friend burns with fever, and a cool cloth helpeth not, he is lost, and you know: then a loved one goeth from your arms, and you, forlorn, learn and find peace.   [5-7-58]

PERMANENCE
Walk on the seashore and your footprints last until the next tide; carve your name in a great rock, and it will last from time to time; move in the sunlight and cast a shadow, and this that you do can outlast the other two.   [1-6-82]

PERSONALITY
Personality is the surface polish of character.   [2-9-56]

PITY
Pity the hurt, share with the needy, but run from a fool lest he crush you.   [6-23-57]

PLANNING
For each there is a place in the great plan, for each there is care and protection.   [5-20-55]

~

Plan you a house, then build; plan you a crop, then plant, for surely none have gone but left plans undone.   [12-30-59]

~

A man plans an elephant hunt for a hide for his sandals, and you who hunt knowledge plan a thousand times a thousand times as for an elephant hunt.   [10-9-61]

~

As you go to the spring for water, you plan the route by bushes; as you travel from city to city, you must travel by the center of the Earth; as one travels to the planets you plan from the center of the Solar system; as the plan of travel may broaden, the center of the galaxy must be located; the constellation may involve its center, and so the center of the Universe must be located.   [11-23-74]

PLEASURE

Pleasure and tears are measured. [5-25-55]

~

One can fill thy cup with fine wine, but a drop of sweat brings greater pleasure. [1-14-64]

~

With care pursue a bear or pleasure, for these be dangerous sports. [3-5-65]

~

Search for the pleasures set aside for you, and use them, lest you be as a sailboat on a great lake without wind for its sails. [9-12-74]

POOR

The poor and the rich oft do small things. [9-11-63]

~

If the poor lose the desire to labor, they have lost their golden flower, their golden flower, and theirs alone. [7-30-79]

POSSESSION

Fill a stump with meat and a hole with wheat and you toil not, for have you not enough? Yet a bear raids the stump and the wheat sprouts. [11-15-58]

~

Your capacity to take and keep plums is limited, as in all things, even gold that is represented by stacked paper. [7-6-59]

~

A hen sitteth upon her egg, and she owns her egg more than man owns his castle. [9-1-59]

~

You may put a latch on a gate, and the latch may hold; but you are a warehouse, a warehouse of gifts, and these you may not hold. [12-2-59]

~

A man with a barn full of wheat can receive no more, and he is as a man whose wife loves him, for surely his barn is full.

[9-28-61]

~

A small space you have, and as you go, you have it.

[4-24-63]

~

Forget not that all you have may be saved for thee by the hands of a stranger. [1-26-78]

POVERTY

Ask another, "Are you poor?" "No," he will answer, "I have bread and a place to sleep!" And if a King cry, "I will feed the poor," he cannot; and he will take from the thrifty and the workers their carriage, and give it to the lazy ones who have no carriages. [12-29-63]

~

Poverty is found in the family of too many for the man to feed; poverty is found by a small stream with too many using it for drink; poverty is found in the city, where men strive to keep their feet out of the mud and huddle from the wind blowing across the prairie where the corn grows high. [2-6-64]

PRAISE

A bit of spice improves the taste of tea; and a word of praise pleases the ear. [12-31-58]

~

A giver of just praise needs to first consider lest his words be soured by waiting. [4-1-59]

~

Take not another's praise, for this angers the body, the mind resists, but the soul careth not. [5-4-59]

~

Cast not rubies to the birds, and words of praise to the undeserving. [9-1-60]

Unjust praise of another may lead to injury to many, and has the face of a lie.   [10-6-64]

PRAYER
Pray, and your prayer will go through the infinite and all eternity.   [1-9-57]

PRAYING
Shout your prayers and you are heard no better; grovel and you obtain dirty knees.   [7-1-58]

PREPARATION
If you climb a steep mountain, first prepare the path of descent; and if you change the heat of the Sun, first plan its restoration.   [1-23-61]

PRESENT
Drop an egg and cry "now," and so mark a part of your present time, a present that joins the past before the egg dries.
[10-24-58]

PRIDE
Pride brings a swagger, a swaggerer is a buffoon, and his face shall lie in the dirt.   [9-7-57]

~

Sit not upon a high post and cry "follow me," lest an egg be cast at thee.   [12-5-58]

~

Show not your fine cloth and vases, for surely the cloth will be dirtied and the vases broken.   [4-6-59]

~

If you would have pride, consider the things that men have done.   [3-24-60]

~

One who buys a fine large horse must buy a silver saddle; and he who rides a large horse on a silver saddle must pay twice over for his grain. [5-6-60]

~

Pride in the actions of men is twenty-five, sorrow equals four; and contentment with place fifty. [11-29-61]

PRIVACY
Guard thy privacy for therein rests your soul; and invade not the privacy of others, for you have no such privilege.

[6-18-57]

~

A dog running in a field has no privacy, an apple tree in an orchard has no privacy; and neither do you, even less.

[9-18-74]

PROBLEMS
Two problems, and the answers are new—the necessity of eating to deliver nutrients to the body—and the necessity of breathing to deliver oxygen to the body. [10-31-74]

~

It is now time to resolve a problem, how to place and pattern explosions so as to move the moon away from the Earth.

[3-4-75]

~

Lest you mourn, lest you thirst, lest you perish know that problems shall be with thee, new to thee but old; so ask, for there has been found the best answer; so ask of others.

[12-16-81]

PROFIT
The quickest and best profit can be realized by the use of knowledge and wisdom in the selection of food for your body.

[1-17-80]

PROGRESS
Progress of man is a strong thing and its course shows strength, and its ends are not set, though it is governed and guided.   [2-17-61]

~

Progress is the high sheen of civilization and comes not from babes, boys or men who stay on beaten trails.   [7-29-64]

~

Progress has two goals at least—to ease or eliminate the daily tasks, or to make a new way for the life affairs of all.
[9-17-78]

~

From the poor and need comes progress in many forms and in great abundance.   [7-30-79]

~

Areas yielding further easy progress will be marked by past successes.   [12-10-79]

PROMISE
Bind your wrists with a silken thread, bind them with chains of fine steel; and if you give a promise or a vow, you are bound and these bonds make the steel chain seem as a silken thread.
[1-10-59]

~

A striking snake and a broken promise have much in common.   [11-30-60]

PROPAGATE
The power to propagate carries not the right.   [5-22-62]

PROPERTY
Those who have much must learn to say no.   [10-19-56]

~

The tail shall follow the dog, and care and prosperity be the same.   [11-25-57]

~

Seize not the property of the newly dead for this seems double thievery.   [9-16-59]

~

If your barn is full of grain, and your field has cattle without number, and your brook is filled with clear water, you are not as a cup that runneth over, for surely you have much more to come that endeth not.   [8-16-63]

PROTECTION

Surely a child has great protection, yet each man hath greater; and it is so.   [5-21-63]

PRUDENCE

A house burns, and a new house is built and it is better; and you survive an adventure, prudence comes and you are better.
                                                           [5-11-59]

PUNISHMENT

Do not interfere with the punishment of the wicked lest you be driven away hurt.   [5-27-55]

~

A white bean is white, and a black bean is black; and a blow is a blow, though called punishment.   [12-9-58]

PURSUIT

The pursuit of meat causes consideration of the time of this pursuing   [2 9 61]

~

Pursuit of bread brings sweat and sweet rest; pursuit of pleasure causes thorn scratches; and pursuit of goodness brings serenity.   [3-1-63]

~

Pursue a toy, a ball, food and lodging, and these you can

secure; but pursue life and you fail; but if you succeed, you will
be first and children will become rare.   [12-29-63]

QUESTIONS
The purest question comes from a child, and deserves that
you exhaust yourself in the answer.   [1-25-65]

REACHING
If you would reach for that which no man has, for that which
never was, look for luck, good or bad; and if you find it, it will
be as salt in soup.   [1-19-63]

REASON
There be three things, men must work, men must propagate,
men must die; and the first two may be reasoned on, for they
are fully known.   [12-8-58]

RECONCILIATION
Reconcile, reconcile and yet again reconcile as greatness is
rare and duties fall there.   [5-3-57]

REGRET
Hammer not a sore toe, nor regret the passing of a happy day
and that you come not this way again, for you hammer a sore
toe with a big hammer, not once but twice.   [9-16-57]

REPUTATION
A bad reputation hangs as a red flag, and comes from sly
remarks of neighbors, from those who magnify faults, and
from courts which have strict rules of evidence.   [8-13-64]

REQUIREMENT
This is too much for this, the list of required things of each
person.   [2-3-60]

RESENTMENT

Resent not the harsh words uttered in anguish, resent not the harsh words uttered in anger; truly resent not, but sorrow; and if you must, depart, and look back again and again. [4-9-57]

~

As a man strives mightily and moves not, another lies pinned to the ground, crushed and bleeding; and each has learned that resentment is a large load to carry, one that one cannot move and that will pin him to the ground, crushed and bleeding.

[9-16-74]

RESPECT

Cast a leaf in the breeze, pop your knuckles, and demand respect, and what gaineth these?—to demand respect is to blow a small whistle. [9-23-57]

REST

A hen lays her eggs in a nest, and this is good; and if you rest, choose a place as good as a hen's nest. [4-9-60]

RESULTS

Lightning cometh again and again and each flash is different, and the results are the same; and people are different and the results of their acts are not the same. [5-21-58]

REWARD

Man has many rewards and few punishments, and the punishments can be listed. [5-15-59]

~

This is a big rock that covers riches   in your leisure hours pursue pleasures that add fine fruit to your just reward for labor well done. [7-10-63]

~

Sudden riches and sudden injury be not always a reward or a

punishment; and the pursuit of reward and the fear of punishment be always present.   [3-5-64]

RICH

He who takes from the rich for others does no good to them
for more than an hour, destroys the incentive for great art, and
acts of skilled charity.   [5-27-79]

RICHES

An heir is given riches; but others earn these and travel
known roads.   [9-9-60]

RIGHTEOUS

The righteous are in a struggle, and their protection is yours;
and the attackers shall retreat and seek the shadows, and the
testing of the righteous is a testing of all.   [2-6-62]

~

Most righteous men speak in a soft voice; and one must seek
and listen.   [9-4-63]

RIGHTNESS

What is right changeth, save a few; and what is wrong is not
the same again and again, save a few.   [11-7-57]

RIGHTS

Pluck a feather from a fowl, and this is but a rustle in the
bushes; take the fur from a fox, and the fox dies; take a right
from a fellow man, and you cannot weigh it.   [4-9-58]

~

A seesaw teetereth the same, the tides come and go and seem
set, and so it is with certain rights and wrongs.   [8-4-58]

~

If an animal attack a man for food, kill it for its necessity and right if less than the right of man; and the right of man exceeds all, even the welfare of the race, if there be such a separate thing.   [10-2-62]

RIPENESS

Watch the fig bush as it ripens and you will find it full of buds.   [6-18-58]

RISING

To rise in the early morning to see flowers refreshed and bathed in the night's dew is a worthy goal.   [9-16-64]

RISK

He who risks his body for money seeks the shade of a dead tree.   [11-21-57]

RIVERS

The day of the running river is about over, as this wastes precipitation, which rules how many live where.   [5-7-80]

SAFETY

Safety cannot be found on a high mountain, behind iron bars and a deep moat; and yet is here for all, and few walk in loose danger save of their own wish.   [6-11-59]

SATISFACTION

A man who becomes satisfied with what he has, that what he has measures him.   [10-22-59]

SAVING

Step not on him who stumbles, but lift him up and he will save thy face.   [12-5-57]

You may save a diamond, with care, though it varies in worth; you may save clothing, with care, for a short while; it is worthwhile to consider the use of that which you save.

[6-6-59]

~

Save not mouldy bread nor sad memories of those who once were and are no more.   [8-24-64]

SAYING

You say "do" and a man is speared; you say "don't" and a widow loses her grain; you say nothing and a man falls in a hole in the ground; and for these you shall receive a blow. [3-4-58]

SEARCHING

A man eats his bread, and this seems an end; a man climbs a ladder, and this seems an end—but it is not so, and the search for an end is frustrating.   [8-3-59]

~

And the search for the rules and means of feeding all men requires more than a little.   [8-3-59]

~

Always there has been a search for facts and knowledge—this search has now been gathered in books—these things for all to see. Many areas have been worked and are quiescent, as there are other places not yet found.

But in the end, all will be found.   [7-14-75]

SECRETS

This is a secret, if there be a secret, and that is that there is none.   [11-12-59]

~

Pick a desert flower and its beauty pleases the eye; and if you find a secret, you can keep it as long as a plucked flower.

[10-17-74]

SEEING

Look around you with your eyes, for it is for you, and no other may see the same. [11-18-58]

~

The record of things that were sheddeth a true light to see the sequences that were, and this aideth, as sequences sometimes recur. [4-10-62]

SEEKING

Seek the reins and the plan that you may never obstruct and always pull the better; and this is your part and is not captivity. [5-21-58]

~

Seek food and raiment and friends, and there is a wafer's difference. [8-9-58]

~

Seek the center, which moves not more than a spear's length, search round and about; seek the edge, and if you reach it, go on a short way, though you may not. [10-10-58]

SELF-ESTEEM

First lace shoes of good leather upon your feet, then a fine feather in your cap. [12-23-59]

SELFISHNESS

Selfishness is surrounded by many hornblowers and each plays a fine tune. [6-13-58]

~

Be kind and careful with the selfish ones, for they are frightened folk, and in their strength know not their ignorance. [5-22-78]

SELF PITY

A blow on thy skull from a small hammer and self-pity do naught for thee. [12-16-64]

SENSES

You live in a darkness for the five senses are incomplete, such as 2 plus 2 equals 4.   [9-2-80]

SEPARATION

Join thy voice in a song with others, and you cannot separate that which you add; nor can you separate that which you do from that which is done by others so that you are wholly one alone.   [12-23-63]

SERVANTS

There have never been better servants paid than the white men of today.   [9-17-64]

SEVENTIES

The greatest event of the decade of the '70's—the demonstration and acceptance of the ability to store human sperm, which can then be used to accomplish normal pregnancy.   [3-26-80]

SHADOWS

A flying bird's shadow leaves a trail on the meadow plain to see, and the Earth is not the same; and if you slap another, the weight of this exceeds the weight of the shadow of the flying bird.   [1-24-64]

SHIELDS

These have no shield: the unlucky ones, who are few, if any; the fated, who are many; and the foolish ones, who stamp.   [10-26-61]

SHIPS

The rudder of a ship is built with care, and the ship goes not a whit except its course is charted, so walk not in a creek.
[8-26-58]

SIN

Sin has a quick profit, and many sins are not punished as a turned page, else there would be none.   [9-20-55]

~

Tell not of the sins of others loosely; but keep it not when duly sought.   [10-19-56]

~

Sin hath a quick compensation, else the weak would not be uncovered.   [4-20-57]

~

A falling leaf taps lightly, and a snake strikes swiftly; and a man laughs at a sin, and the penalty makes the strike of the snake as the tap of a falling leaf.   [11-7-58]

~

An elephant wallows in a swamp and leaves a hole for all to see; and the sign of a sin is as an elephant wallow.   [2-23-59]

~

If you go on a trail, and it be wrong, even though food and time and labor have been used, yet you must turn to the right trail; and if a friend commits a sin, for sure, you must depart if you cannot first aid him, and he repents not.   [5-5-59]

~

A trail coated with ice is hard to travel, and a tall cliff can be climbed, and do these, if you must, to correct a sin. [2-12-60]

~

In the war against sin, each fights a lonely fight; and is surrounded by much help.   [5-15-63]

~

If you have a sin, you will attract others who have a sin, and

they will encircle you; and if you break not out, you will be crushed into the Earth and will produce only a small stink.
[11-20-63]

SKIN

Your skin resists not the slash of a knife, so cover it, lest it lie open.
[8-27-58]

SLEEP

The need for sleep varies from person to person, age to age, place to place, and time to time, and serves best the sick, lazy and fearful.
[1-16-75]

SMALLNESS

The small man carries a knife overly sharp; the big man carries a heavy weight minute by minute.
[10-31-57]

~

A small bit you are; yet, a small bit you are, and this smallness is mighty though made of small bits that must hang together.
[4-24-63]

SMILES

Pin not a rose on a bush and a smile on your face, as the rose will surely die and your face will tire.
[10-16-57]

~

A smile adorns better than a cut rose.
[6-2-61]

~

Match a smile with a smile and it is doubled.
[3-20-80]

SORROW

Sorrow and regret have depths and shallowness, and pass, and of these regret is the faster.
[8-2-57]

~

First run a short mile, then a long mile; carry a small load, then a heavy square load, so it is with sorrow. [4-19-58]

~

If you see a crooked foot, sorrow not; and a friend sickens and dies, despair not; and a storm sweeps many people to sea and they are lost, fear not; for surely you know not what makes the grass grow green. [4-19-61]

~

When another is stricken, your sorrow is best expressed by the aid you give. [10-5-74]

~

The heat of change and living distill joy and happiness away; and the residue is called sorrow. [7-14-75]

~

Sorrow is like a dark cloud that yields rain which cleans the air and good water to drink, then drifts away, never to be seen again. [2-4-80]

SOUNDNESS

Surely sound men are better formed and found oftener than blossoms on a peach tree. [3-14-61]

SPEAKING

Speak softly, and but a little, when a mistake plagues you, lest an echo overdin you. [8-29-57]

SPECULATION

For diversion presume:
1. That time has moved six thousand years;
2. That the waters of the ocean have remained still, the sun has shone, that oxygen has remained sufficient;
3. That men have continued to do as they listed.

Now speculate upon housing, communication, travel, and the structure of men after centuries of controlled procreation.

[6 21 61]

STRENGTH

The cock crows and a strong man fails his test; and the cock crows again, and the test is less.   [10-15-57]

~

Learn your strength, consider the broken bone, and keep an iron measure well worn.   [12-5-57]

~

A peach and an apple are not the same; and some men are stronger than others, and any who resent this cannot see the beauty of the moon.   [7-31-59]

~

A strong man can carry a large load and climb a hill; but a weaker one plus another does this better.   [2-17-61]

~

If a sudden flood entraps you, and you find a great rock, rest upon the rock until the flood ebbs; and in a sudden flood in life, a strong man is better than a great rock.   [11-15-61]

~

The strength of the strong is the strength of the nation; and the weakness of the weak must not pull down the strong.   [11-2-62]

STRUTTING

A rooster crows and struts; and the one who struts in front of a gathering and makes noise with his mouth, does less than a rooster.   [5-15-58]

STUTTERING

A stuttering man causes mirth, and proves he is a man, only doubly so.   [4-7-62]

SUBSTANCE

If a wounded deer fall upon the plain, the vultures gather and feed; and lay not your substance out as a fallen deer, for the idle and profligate will feed as vultures.   [4-2-60]

SUICIDE

If you would add six to six, eleven is a close answer but a wrong one; suicide is a wrong one; suicide is a wrong answer to any problem, and is not close.   [7-31-63]

SUN

The rain falls on all, and the wind wanders freely over the land, and all have darkness when the sun goes down.
[1-21-58]

~

The sun shines upon a high peak, and the sun shines in the sky that all men may see; and it too is part and it yields its use.
[2-13-58]

~

He who seeth the sun rise and says day is coming is right; and you can say I will go there, and go; you prophesy, and a few may do more.   [9-11-58]

SUSPICION

Smoke rises into the faces round about the fire; and suspicion rises from a wrong and covers those round and about and then it too blows away.   [5-5-59]

SWEAT

Sweat and birth juices should be washed away that the new be new.   [9-20-57]

~

The sweat of humans would make two small oceans, it measures progress, and yet no hero of this sweat brigade has received as much as a tin medal.   [1-21-80]

SYMPATHY

Give not sympathy to one who has lost a finger, for he has nine others; nor to a man who has lost a foot, for there is yet another: but give to a fool, for he is hungry, thirsty and knoweth not from whence cometh the cold North wind.   [9-15-81]

TALK

Cook not your meat too much, nor smarten yourself overly so, lest your talk has no listeners.   [8-5-58]

TAKING

Take not from the desperate that which he hath, for this cannot be good, though you may buy it at a double fair price.
[3-16-57]

~

Take not from a fool that which is his, though he cannot keep it and shall lose it, or let it rust away.   [3-16-57]

~

Seize not a ripe grape, it crushes; seize not an egg of a hen, it crushes; seize not gold, its weight is a burden; but take gently, ever so gently, from things that surround thee.   [10-8-62]

~

Thy taking you consider, but consider also your losing that which you take.   [9-17-63]

TEACHERS

A teacher is unlike a coconut that hath only so much milk and no more; a teacher has much, has fresh material each day.
[7-3-59]

TEARS

Weep, and a tear may reach the Earth; cry out, and you may be heard for a mile, no more.   [1-9-57]

~

Howl not in trouble, but cry softly and all will bring aid.
[2-26-57]

~

The outcries of childbirth and the tears of a new widow come, and the tears soil not the Earth and the outcries have no echo. [10-14-63]

TEMPTATION

All shall be adequately tempted and shall be as peeled fruit.
[9-20-55]

~

Temptation serves a purpose, as all else. [1-20-56]

~

A woman carries a baby only so long, and this is known, and it is known that temptation shows the cracked. [2-10-60]

THEFT

A thief steals and this is a theft; but a smart one who taketh unfairly from the less smart does a heavy theft. [4-3-64]

THIEF

If a thief steals your purse and spends your coins and is caught, beat him not but give him more coins and let him go.
[11-21-61]

THINGS

The things you have, you truly have not, so use them while you may; and your power to use passes and is not steady.
[7-12-57]

~

There are things that were and always have been; there are things that were, and are not; there are things to be that are not now. [2-2-59]

THOUGHT

Spend your coins idly, build a home of mud, but let not a thought vanish. [2-19-58]

~

A flame burneth brightly, and thoughts without number enter; and the useful come forth hardened and the faulty are consumed. [2-28-62]

THREATS

If a cloud filled with lightning and hail cometh, seek shelter and stand fast; and if you receive a threat, seek shelter and stand fast. [3-11-59]

THUNDER

Thunder rumbles through the sky, avalanches roar, earthquakes race across the plains and shake great cities; but these be small compared to the thud of a man's bare foot on a fresh plowed field. [8-7-61]

TIME

A picture is time frozen. [9-20-55]

~

Practice as a beginner on "what is a moment?" [1-25-56]

~

He who counts the wing beats of a sparrow as it flies from tree to tree has not time to plant the seed to raise a crop to feed the mouth. [9-21-59]

~

Anger, sickness and a black cloud filled with hail and rain cost you time. [1-28-60]

~

One can measure time by the hour, the day and the year; but full time is measureless. [10-3-60]

~

Your tracks in the sand by the sea are clear and strong, and, yet, after an hour are gone and the sadness is wiped away by the knowledge that this is right.   [9-28-64]

~

If you would gain one more day of life, you would burn many fields of ripening grain and forests of trees full with large branches, so waste not a moment of any day for it is worth a field of ripening grain and a mighty tree full of large branches.   [8-22-74]

~

If you would laugh, you must first laugh—
If you would cry, you will cry—
And if you idle your time away, you shall both laugh and cry.
                    [1-19-78]

TOMORROW
Ding Dong
The men of tomorrow shall truly say of us, "They lived crudely."
Ding Dong
And the men of the morrow's tomorrow shall say, "They lived crudely."
Ding Dong
And the end of this is not in sight.
Ding Dong   [1-3-63]

TRAGEDY
An orange turns red, an apple turns round, and these be true tragedy.   [4 19 60]

TRAVELING
A long road climbing into the mountains tires the traveler; and he who looks into the future becomes as a tired traveler who finds a green valley.   [8-29-60]

TREMBLING

The stars tremble when a strong man trembles.   [7-10-64]

TROUBLE

Have not little troubles in a big way.   [10-6-55]

~

Bear little troubles, share big troubles sparingly lest your friends be overburdened, though big troubles belong not to you alone.   [4-30-57]

~

Signs and rain and trouble are about upon the Earth, and you may depart from them though troubles sticketh. [8-8-57]

~

Flick your sweat into the ocean, cast your tears on the desert sands, and so mark the passing troubles.   [12-16-57]

~

Run and nothing happens, and your troubles are meted out and received.   [5-15-58]

~

A man's hat and shoes fit as a well-made jacket and so do his troubles.   [2-13-63]

TRUST

Pour not vinegar into your milk, nor darken the light given by trust, for trust enables you to walk more easily. [7-29-57]

~

It payeth little, breaketh easily, and mendeth slowly for the trust of another is as a bird's egg on your shoulder. [11-7-57]

TRUTH

There is one thing that never hurts, the truth; and this is one among many things that never hurt.   [12-23-59]

~

Save a child from a storm; but more than this, aid a man that he speak the truth.   [4-18-60]

~

A man asks, "Is it a brown calf?" Answer true, "It is a brown calf with five white spots," for he is a helper against the cold and is entitled to ask and have the full truth, lest he fall.
[6-13-61]

TRYING

You may try, and cannot: it will be spoken, and you will not hear; you may try, but he who does not, yet may.   [10-31-57]

UNITY

All join hands and repel an attack by a wolf pack and find and use the strength of unity.   [12-18-58]

UNIVERSE

All in the Universe is enclosed in a sack that came from a large corridor—a corridor wider by a third than its height; and the sack was a sixth of its width.

This corridor has an atmosphere, not of our air, and was lit by a pervading light, and the end could not be seen.

This sack was opened at the top and all was dumped in at one time. This sack cannot be opened from within, and nothing here can penetrate this sack.   [9-19-74]

~

The year 1977 had one great event—an effort was begun to inventory and chart the bodies in the Universe.   [1-2-78]

~

We have encountered through the ages and countless times another form of life in the Universe and it has resulted in religions.   [6-16-78]

UNTRUTH

Let the sun shine and the darkness go for truth and untruth seemeth so.   [12-27-57]

USE

The claw of the tiger severs; the cut hair falls to the ground and blows about, and is used; and there is naught that serves not.   [4-8-58]

VALUE

Birds drink from a stream, fish find life there and it shines in the sun, and it has high value; but many find a greater value in a polished stone.   [5-1-61]

VANITY

Carry a square brick and a heavy pound of lead, and you receive pay, yet vanity overweighs these and is acid and there is no profit.   [12-20-57]

VICTORIES

Quiet victories by unacclaimed warriors—quiet victories of unmeasured worth in the great struggle for survival. This great struggle that overrides every other thing and into which all are thrust, has inflicted total defeat and destruction without exception.

And now many cross the boundary of seventy years, walking firmly, with sound minds and bodies.

Quiet victories over disease and malfunction and now the boundary is passed and the light shines afar.

But victories continue and the war for survival will be totally won.   [4-28-75]

~

While many victories have occurred in the War of Survival in which all are warriors, victory will come from bits of wisdom gained by fresh levies.   [4-21-78]

~

Small victories have been gained in the struggles to avoid and overcome gravity, the climate, and variance in the land masses.   [4-10-80]

VIOLENT
If you go with the violent and in the mud, resent not the blows and the mud on your boots.   [3-8-62]

VISION
A ray of light strikes a cloud and gives a burst of color in the sky for all and awe to him who truly sees.   [6-13-61]

VOICES
The waves of the sea run high, are green and are not the same; the flakes of snow in the air form drifts and are not the same; the trees of the jungle reach to the sky and receive not the same shine of the sun; and the voices of men are large and small, and are not equal in all things.   [2-18-58]

~

A drop of rain clatters down into a cascading rapid which makes a loud roar; and the voice of a man when joined with others becomes as a cascading roar.   [6-21-61]

WAITING
One who waits loses the light from his candle.   [7-26-57]

~

You wait for this, for that and the other; but fret not as this is but gentle practice for the big wait.   [5-4-82]

WANTS
A biting dog bites again, and is destroyed; beware of your wants for they make you as a biting dog.   [8-29-59]

WARMTH
If a nation burns its coal and trees it has a quick warmth, but a long coldness.   [12-8-64]

WARNING

If a stranger curse you, it is more than the braying of a donkey in the field, and this is the first; if a friend chide you, and then leaves, it is the second; and if a good man looks at you, says nothing, but chooses another path, this is the third warning; and you must amend yourself.   [3-29-60]

WASTE

Waste not on wasted years, for this is waste.   [7-24-57]

~

Cast aside the hiss from between your teeth, but naught else wastefully.   [3-23-58]

~

If you would look for waste, look among the things used by men.   [4-3-63]

WAYWARDNESS

Wayward ones find lack of shade and tell tales of hard stone.
                    [5-20-55]

WEAKNESS

The weak hide behind the strong; and a laughing liar shoveth forward an honest man.   [6-3-58]

WEALTH

The wealth of the world is limitless and is a testing tool of men who are to be tested at any moment, and the tests are full.
                    [5-20-55]

~

Wealth flows not as the currents of the waters and the winds of the air.   [6-2-61]

~

If you have great wealth, you can have many coats that you need not; and you can give to the poor who will say, "He is a rich man and it is nothing."   [10-17-74]

WELFARE
Take care of the welfare of the individual for the general
welfare has its sure foundation here.   [3-21-82]

WICKEDNESS
The wicked come from the imperfect, and the good remain
imperfect.   [4-20-57]
~

Put not another stone on the load of the wicked, but stand
clear, lest you be contaminated.   [5-31-57]
~

Think not on the joys of wickedness as this is a high cliff.
[1-18-58]

WIND
A cold wind howls in the night, and you call another a name
which he likes not; and he will like it worse than the cold wind
howling in the night.   [11-19-58]

WISDOM
Limited wisdom is wise, for a boy cannot make cloth.
[9-20-55]
~

Each living thing for a time shall have a sufficiency, even of
wisdom.   [6-6-57]
~

The stars shine, and the light is small, and a friend giveth an
apple and this is small; and the moon giveth more light, and
you receive a house which lasts longer; and the sun shines and
lights the whole world, and a word of wisdom lasts forever.
[4-3-58]
~

Rattle not a pea in a pod lest you drown out the voice of a
wise man as a wise man speaks softly.   [6-6-58]
~

The wise man gains respect, the wiser man gains respect and love, and the wisest makes silence, has humility and giveth freely.   [6-10-58]

~

Another gives you food and of his wisdom, and of these his wisdom is best, even though of old.   [7-15-58]

~

Wisdom washes away chance-taking as a strong soap.   [12-4-58]

~

A man can measure his well and know how much water he has, and he can measure his fence; but no man can measure the wisdom of another.   [7-28-59]

~

The Sun shines alone and is sufficient; and if you uncover a shortage in the Earth, you but uncover a shortage of wisdom.   [6-31-60]

~

It is better to flaunt ermine before others than wisdom.   [10-25-60]

~

Walk barefoot on the earth, gaze on its width, wonder and wander on the rose-covered paths if you would extend man's wisdom an iota.   [6-5-61]

~

An open bucket catches rain, and be as an open bucket for wisdom that falls freely as rain.   [6-13-61]

~

Human wisdom and intelligence are best displayed and used in the curing of human bodies.   [1-22-75]

~

The wisdom of the human race is soon to be tested as it faces the necessity of issuing permits for children.   [3-27-75]

~

The young have not wisdom, and know it not—those in their

middle years know its absence—and all must listen with an
open mind, for it will come as a strange tale.   [1-26-78]

~

The young shall have freely and fully of the wisdom of the
older ones.   [6-26-78]

~

A great thing with many hopeless victories—gathering and
using the assembled wisdom of many.   [3-31-82]

WOMAN

A racial law—cherish the pregnant woman.   [3-28-63]

~

Two things this year—the fear of disease and the fear of
pregnancy—have gone from women.   [7-10-64]

~

Help the young woman who has fallen, for her way is hard
and her strength is small.   [7-10-64]

WORDS

A great stone falleth heavily, great waters wash deep, and a
harsh word drives souls away.   [12-8-57]

~

A small cut on the skin cures in seven days and causes a small
moan; but a hasty word etches the memory and aches and
aches.   [1-6-59]

~

Shun hot words as they sear friends, who may leave and
return not; and these be doubly hot in the heat of Summer.
[8-25-63]

~

A stone fence lasts for centuries, a stone house serves for
generations, yet when a man speaks a loving word to a son, it
goes into the love of the race and lasts forever.   [1-28-64]

WORK

The opportunity to work is full and free to all.   [5-27-55]

~

The worker may be content, if his chains are of gold.
[3-26-56]

~

All workers have always been paid fully, and this leads to
this—no worker works for men.   [7-21-59]

~

The light you see by is not a true light, and the firm ground
upon which you walk is not truly firm, yet you may see the
bricks and mortar set out for the work of the tomorrows and
find no place for you.   [10-16-59]

~

A pecan is a pecan and nothing fills its place; and the law of
work exists and outlasts all pecans.   [1-4-60]

~

He who takes my work takes my clothes and leaves me
stripped, leaves my cupboard bare, takes my shoes and I must
walk barefoot in the cold.   [9-28-81]

WORRY

Wear a heavy shoe and step not on a hot cinder. [6-20-58]

~

A lion's bite and worry do thee little good:
1. Consider and accept the growth pattern of the body, and
   it varies not;
2. Stand on your feet and measure the distance of the area
   where mostly you shall live;
3. Compute the years you will have, and thus a worry area
   fades away.   [11-13-63]

WORTH

Each man, even the cripple who stumbles in the street, is

worth more than the gold in the river and the eagle which soars on high.   [4-1-61]

~

Thy worth is endless and improveth.   [2-28-62]

~

Test the worth of what you do with "Does it improve the circumstances of living?"   [5-30-63]

~

Your worth to yourself, family and neighbors is set by what you do, and your rewards come from worth.   [3-3-75]

~

Which is greater:
Cool shelter is now available to the many from the heat of the hot summer sun—it is now announced that the hunt for the bacteria causing smallpox is successfully completed and all are now destroyed.   [9-4-78]

WRONGS

Belabor not the matter, some wrongs will remain wrong until changed, and then all will know.   [12-12-56]

~

To join in wrong is to walk on sharp rocks.   [11-16-57]

~

An unjustly wronged one is overcompensated ere the day is done.   [8-4-58]

~

Wrong is known, right may need seeking; but many things are neither and these bounce, hop, jump and run freely; and if one of these bounces on your head, it will cut deeply, leave a scar, and the hair will grow there no more.   [8-26-61]